SOME CANNOT BE CAUGHT
THE EMMA PRESS BOOK OF BEASTS

OTHER TITLES FROM THE EMMA PRESS

POETRY ANTHOLOGIES

The Emma Press Anthology of the Sea
This Is Not Your Final Form: Poems about Birmingham
The Emma Press Anthology of Aunts
The Emma Press Anthology of Love

BOOKS FOR CHILDREN

Moon Juice, by Kate Wakeling
The Noisy Classroom, by Ieva Flamingo
The Queen of Seagulls, by Rūta Briede
The Book of Clouds, by Juris Kronbergs

PROSE PAMPHLETS

Postcard Stories, by Jan Carson
First fox, by Leanne Radojkovich
The Secret Box, by Daina Tabūna
Me and My Cameras, by Malachi O'Doherty

POETRY PAMPHLETS

Dragonish, by Emma Simon
Pisanki, by Zosia Kuczyńska
Who Seemed Alive & Altogether Real, by Padraig Regan
Paisley, by Rakhshan Rizwan

THE EMMA PRESS PICKS

The Dragon and The Bomb, by Andrew Wynn Owen
Meat Songs, by Jack Nicholls
Birmingham Jazz Incarnation, by Simon Turner
Bezdelki, by Carol Rumens

SOME CANNOT BE CAUGHT

THE EMMA PRESS BOOK OF BEASTS

Edited by Anja Konig
and Liane Strauss

THE EMMA PRESS

First published in Great Britain in 2018 by the Emma Press Ltd

Poems copyright © individual copyright holders 2018
Selection copyright © Anja Konig and Liane Strauss 2018

All illustrations created by Emma Wright from images found on Early English Books Online (EEBO).

All rights reserved.

The right of Anja Konig and Liane Strauss to be identified as the editors of this work has been asserted by them in accordance with the Copyright, Designs and Patents Act 1988.

ISBN 978-1-910139-88-2

A CIP catalogue record of this book is available
from the British Library.

Printed and bound in Great Britain
by TJ International, Padstow.

The Emma Press
theemmapress.com
queries@theemmapress.com
Jewellery Quarter, Birmingham, UK

EDITORS' INTRODUCTION

Anja: Humans are animals. I have long found this a clarifying thought. There is much we have in common, most importantly the desire to belong to the herd, which is the hallmark of any social species. As with other social animals, we pay a price for this belonging: our obsession with hierarchy, with knowing who is top dog; power structures, pecking orders. The human animal is capable of competition and collaboration, aggression and love.

Liane: And of course, humans are not the only animals who form friendships, are capable of selflessness and can act out of the desire to help others. Recent research confirms that 'monkeys, apes, dogs, and a growing list of other mammals, can recognize and protest unfair conditions'. Not only this, but: 'Animals employ various forms of punishment… [that bear a] striking resemblance to our most effective modes of rehabilitative and restorative justice.'[1]

You might say science is finally catching up to what poets at least as far back as Aesop have always known, that the boundary lines humans like to draw between other animals and themselves are far more elastic, and porous, than they think.

Anja: The anthology explores these fluid lines of separation between us and other animals, speaking about empathy for others of our own kind as well as animals of different species. A beautiful example is Maggie Sawkins' 'Frilled Lizard':

> *he may be cold to the touch*
>   *but inside*
> *he's alight*

Liane: You can see those lines dissolving in Maggie Dietz's 'Late spring', where 'the boy' sitting in his bath identifies with 'the vanished bird' and sees them both, merged, in the mock-heroic simile: 'The soft pink belly like a clam.'

Anja: But the book also speaks of the limits of empathy, of cruelty and indifference, of predators and prey, like Russell Jones's 'The Alligator Get-Out Clause':

> *When it moves, don't resist –*
> *the alligator has spent millennia perfecting its bite.*

Liane: Speaking of jaws and clauses, quite a few of the poems sink their teeth into the question of language, whether it really is one of the things that separates humans from other beasts.

Anja: Yes, that's a common theme in the anthology. Did you notice how in Pascale Petit's 'My Wolverine', for instance, 'words are born/ fighting'?

Liane: I sure did! There's also a telephone receiver in that poem that acts like a muzzle. And I felt my own blood run cold when the response to the words 'barked' in Saliann St-Clair's 'You smell like apples' evolves from an instinctive repulse to deliberate violence.

Anja: So the poems examine how we as humans are similar to animals and how we are, or think we are, different from them. The poems speak to what is shared – joy, fear, aggression, sex.

Liane: Yes, and humour. Don't forget humour. My favourite rhyme in the book is the one Nancy Campbell comes up with for the new mammal whose discovery she celebrates, very much à la Dorothy Parker, in 'The Omnivore'.

Anja: The most intense pleasure for the editor of an anthology is the dialogue with other poets, the thrill of reading submissions and finding the poem that jolts you, that addresses you, that shows you how it's done.

Liane: Absolutely. I was dazzled by the economy with which Stav Poleg collapses the putative boundary between civilisation and nature in the opening image of 'Boy':

> *The most unlikely fish,*
> *swimming upright like a streetlamp*
>
> *in an ocean.*

Anja: It was electrifying to read Sarah Hesketh's 'Martha, The Last Passenger Pigeon', a topic that has long fascinated me; she wrote the poem I wanted to write, wrote it perfectly and wrote it in a way that I never would have in a million years: Martha, the endling of her species, as a good-time girl:

> *Lipstick fires in her feathers; the smoky*
> *turn of her neck as she came into a room.*
> *Who knew where she was going to, and*
> *what's a girl like that got to do with settling down?*

Liane: Like Martha, every poem in this anthology knows 'how to make a party swing'!

Anja and Liane: Well, we could talk about these poems until the cows come home – but I guess it's time to take our cue from Martha and make an endling by saying some thank yous. First of all, we want to thank everybody at the Emma Press for giving us the opportunity to co-edit this anthology and for putting this beautiful book together.

Liane: I want to thank you, Anja, for approaching me with this idea in the first place!

Anja: And I want to thank you, Liane, for expanding my horizons – together we made this a much more interesting anthology than it would have been with a single editor!

Liane and Anja: Finally, we want to say a mammoth thank you to the 300 plus poets from all over the world who sent us more than 800 poems about monkeys, dogs, goats, chickens, people, a frilled lizard, a passenger pigeon, a zebra in New York, the pangolin, scorpions, lemurs, snowfleas, giraffes, flamingos, ladybirds, lapwings, horseshoe crabs, a hare in a boxing ring, a bear on a bicycle, alligators, rabbits, foxes, a slug, a fossa and an olinguito. They made it very hard to choose, but we had a fantastic journey discovering all their work and assembling this anthology together! We feel sure that every reader who dives into these poems will find something rich and strange – and return to their all-too-human lives 'with salt in their hair'.

ANJA KONIG AND LIANE STRAUSS

[1] Nathan H. Lents, The Human Evolution Blog. https://thehumanevolutionblog.com/2016/10/14/the-biological-foundations-of-justice/

CONTENTS

The Alligator Owns The Pool

Gorilla, by Mel Pryor	1
I Had a Brindled Cow, Anonymous	2
The Flood Committee, by Victoria Briggs	4
Late spring, by Maggie Dietz	5
'You smell like apples', by Saliann St-Clair	7
My Wolverine, by Pascale Petit	9
Harvest, by Gregg Friedberg	10
Boy, by Stav Poleg	13
The Alligator Get-Out Clause, by Russell Jones	15
Scorpion, by Sharon Black	16
The Lemures, by Abigail Parry	17
The Incredible Mrs Fox, by Angela Readman	18
The Omnivore, by Nancy Campbell	20

The Whole King Kong Experience

Frilled Lizard, by Maggie Sawkins	23
Documentary on the Pangolin, by Jon Stone	24
Slug, by Sandra Horn	26
i, scarab, by Gabrielle Turner	28
Fossa, by Pascale Petit	30
Zebra on East 55th and 3rd, by Ian Humphreys	33
Snowflea Migration, by Philip Fried	34
Pond Requiem, by Cheryl Moskowitz	35
Lesser flamingo, by Donika Kelly	38

Ladybird, by Emma McKervey 39
Lapwings in Fallowfield, by Katherine Horrex 41
Romance in New Jersey, by Kathleen Moran Bainbridge 42

Fins That Could Be Wings

Hare, by Pauline Plummer 45
Macbeth, by Eve Lacey 46
Build, by Susan Richardson 47
The Zoo Keeper's Song, by Maggie Sawkins 49
Family Viewing, by Jacqueline Saphra 50
The Fish without a Bicycle, by Shauna Robertson 53
Ordeal by Water, by Helen Ivory 54
Reynard, by Ruth Wiggins 55
How d'ya like them apples? by Rosie Shepperd 56
Myxomatosis, 1970s, by Tim Cresswell 57
Are we there yet? by Maggie Dietz 58
Kyril's Tale, by David Hale 60
Chimpanzee Burial at Sanaga-Yong Rescue Centre, by Degna Stone 62
Martha, The Last Passenger Pigeon, by Sarah Hesketh 64

..

Acknowledgements 67
About the editors 69
About the authors 70
About the Emma Press 76

PART 1
The Alligator Owns The Pool

Gorilla

You could sense expectation, the kids at the cage
after the whole King Kong experience,
a pecs-bashing, jungle titan performance
from the attraction, sprawled across the floor
like a discarded coat. A crowd of boys
plopped mints like mothballs through the bars, to lure
a look, a rise; the body lumbering,
on hands and knees it seemed, to centre stage,
the beaten stance and cowed, obedient eyes
still holding their magnificence. I thought
I'd found a new dawn of Darwin, I thought
I'd found the origin of suffering,
would've put my cheek against his long malaise,
said brother, forefather, I *know* what this is.

ANONYMOUS

I Had a Brindled Cow

I had a brindled cow,
Sheltered in the byre.
What became of the brindled cow?
I traded her for money.
What became of the money?
The river swept it away.
What became of the river?
Black bulls lapped it up.
What became of the black bulls?
They vanished down a long road.
What became of the long road?
It was overgrown by madder.
What became of the madder?
Young girls picked the flowers.
What became of the girls?
They rode away with young men.
What became of the young men?
They lived in manors beyond the hills.
What became of the manors?
They all went up in blue flames,
They dwindled down to ashes.
What became of the pile of ashes?
A black hen raked it away.
What became of the black hen?
A hawk carried her off.
What became of the hawk?
He vanished over green groves.

What became of the green groves?
The sons of God felled the trees.
What became of the sons of God?
They climbed up into the sky,
Strumming strings, drumming drums.
What are they doing in the sky?
They sit behind a table writing –
Who shall die, who shall live,
On this earth beneath the sun.

**TRANSLATED FROM LATVIAN
BY BITITE VINKLERS**

'I Had a Brindled Cow' belongs to the traditional Latvian folk songs known as the *dainas*, handed down orally from generation to generation. Collected primarily in the late nineteenth century and numbering over 30,000 texts, they are included in the UNESCO Memory of the World Register. The poem is probably a winter solstice song, when predictions were made about life and death in the coming year.

The Flood Committee

The cat is hosting secret salons
with the songbird. Peace talks
beneath the hawthorn bush
in a language neither mew nor purr
nor the siren-savage warble he
saves for others of his kind.

He chatters now in sweet vibrato,
a pidgin trill the songbird looks as if she
understands, at least one note in every three.

Cat's paws are pom-poms, the claws retracted
his arms laid down on forest floor.

Soon the dog will come to join them and
after that, the sheep, the horse. A flood committee,
who read the signs and own the blueprints
and resolve, this time, to keep
us out the Ark.

Late spring

In a bath with baking soda the boy pondered
the vanished bird: spindly wings netted with veins,
tufts of fuzz at the wattled throat, the skin there
pink and feathered as an old man's neck
or hand. Black eyes visible through skeins
of lids. The soft pink belly like a clam.

Later he'd dream of swimming in air without
a float or wings, of a raw chicken in a pot
of wine and herbs, and the bald neighbour
who spoke by holding a box to his throat.

It had dropped from the elm to the driveway.
The boy had watched it whine and rasp,
then fetched a flour sack and his doctor's kit.

The scalding water pinked his skin, pruned
his finger bulbs so that he couldn't see the whorls.
His mother dipped a toothbrush in acetone,
scrubbed beneath the child's transparent nails.

She put the boy to bed, the bandaged bird,
expired, between the fence and garden shed,
the toy stethoscope in a bowl of bleach –
clean of its work, its good intentions.

All night, the elm swam in its net of stars.
Disease would take it and the neighbour
but not that summer, not that night.

The boy swam circles around the old man's
metal lawn chair. The chicken danced
in its savoury bath and the old man sang like
a gramophone or robot *so remember this, life is no abyss,*
somewhere there's a bluebird of happiness as green crabapples
plunked from the branches onto macadam.

'You smell like apples'

was the first thing he barked at me.
That's what conversations with him were like,
an attack – like a pest, one with wings, *incoming* –
that the attackee would bat away from their ears,
instinctively at first, then on purpose.
He was a tick.
Needy, latching on – but he didn't seem to know it.
I kept my expression quiet, and my body neutral –
playing dead keeps most predators at bay.
It was quiet. We all knew. He: the last to.

Realisation rearranged his balance and steamed up his face with anger, and not just regular anger either but the kind marinating in shame.

Peacocking drove his actions – entitlement akin to plumage. He had a list with check marks on it – a very long one that he carried around behind his zip. We are all on the list.

You (they) are easy to spot because they (you) have a persistent unalterable uniform, and a *please notice me* desperate stench on them like skin is worn. Lone wolves, or running in packs; gaggles of men intent on nourishing themselves with, at the very least, glances that equal a way in.

His glance was *my* way in.

He cleared his throat, twice, then coughed into the hole he made with his fist and cleared his throat again. It wasn't enough, so he did a pull-up. He wasn't above this.

In the train window's reflection, my eyes *were* all over him like skin is worn.

My Wolverine

When my mother says I was her kit
taken from her too early,
I think not of cats but a wolverine,
my devourer of snowfields, who,
when she can find no more prey,
eats herself, even the frozen bones.
I crawl down the black phone line
as if it's an umbilicus
to the last refuge on our planet,
towards whatever back country
happens to be her territory today.
My nails remember to claw.
I lope up the icefall
she's retreated to, that's melting behind her
as she climbs her precipice, too drunk
on freedom to come down.
She shows me the den where words are born
fighting. I do not blame her.
I hold the receiver against my face
as if it's her muzzle, her reek
of blizzard-breath. I embrace
the backward-barbed teeth that can
fell a moose and gnaw even its hooves.
Kit – she spits the word out
in a half-love half-snarl and I
am her glutton, scavenging on my yelp
when I was torn from her after birth,
and again now – not long before she dies.

GREGG FRIEDBERG

Harvest

The boughs sagged.
The ground swelled.

I'd planted no garden,
but now it was harvest time.

Bees had beaten me
to the pears. I sidled
into a bower of fraught boughs
that closed in

as the bees gloved each next fruit
in their rife numbers.

So were it better
to unearth onions?

One lay peeled and pale
on a raised bed.

Then I realised:
you were watching me.

Not as you are
but as you're ripening to be.

'Cheat!' you screeched,
an eye glowering

in the deep shade, reached,
grasped a bough, shook it hard,

loosed a squall of fruit and bees
you meant to be

the end of me.

Boy

The most unlikely fish,
swimming upright like a streetlamp

in an ocean.
I'd love to say

when I first learned you were a seahorse
everything

                                    fell into place.
How you'd been curled into the circles

of your spine –
breathing bubbles into your paper-cut

slow skin.
I'd love to say I've always understood

the hesitation
                 of your water-pace,

your cellophane-like fins
       that could be wings,

or once were wings,
       the most unlikely Pegasus.

Once upon a time
there was a seahorse – a yellow seahorse –

a little lemon bubble
like a curl of light and rain.

>   But now that my palm is as flat
>   as the ocean –

>   >   I'll follow
>   >   your footprints

instead.

The Alligator Get-Out Clause

Pre-history, an evil eye, sinister-sleek
mississippiensis, walking Appalachian,
taut, primed to roll, a grizzled submarine.

The alligator owns the pool, the 18 holes,
the bayou, parking lot, riverside. Beware
your trespass: ancient, hungry, vacant,

the alligator does not care about your kids,
your direct debits, cholesterol, insurance wavers.
The alligator does not know forgiveness,

is inhumanly patient. Long and quiet, you cease
in its alien eyes. When it moves, don't resist –
the alligator has spent millennia perfecting its bite.

Scorpion

for Gaia, born November 3rd

You appeared under the shower spray
like an auspice. My contact lenses
not yet in place, I thought you were a clump of hair,
a rubber washer, a fallen clasp
just visible beneath my full moon belly,
already contracting.

Squatting, I saw six black hinges,
pincers neat as needlework raised
as if mid-stitch,
your tail curled up – not, as I thought,
primed to strike
but a hook for a finger to lift it from the basin.

We faced each other through the steam,
both in that instant unafraid
yet deadly to the other –
you scuttled off before presence of mind
made me scream through to the next room
where you were not yet born.

Sweet little nipper,
polished onyx, precious brooch.
Six hours later, worn out,
blood still fresh between my legs,
I fastened you to my breast.

ABIGAIL PARRY

The Lemures

Something is digging the stuffing from the old red plush
of the seat behind you in the darkened theatre.
And later, with the rain falling not-quite-right
in the headlights, and the odd half-glimpsed zigzag,
and the cat's eyes coming unstuck, that soft tug-
tugging at your collar grows insistent: they are still here.

Still here, with their quick fingers and luminous eyes,
their spook faces, their fingers hooked like questions.
You meet them half way, know them from halfway places –
the empty A-road, the mezzanine, the bent
reflection in the lift doors before they purr
open again on the things you know: phones ringing, people.

They are a nuisance. They have so many questions
and no respect for the living. They prod and pinch,
they stare. They paw at the glass between what is yours
and what is theirs. Do not feed them – they will always
want more. They will steal from you. Pickpockets,
rifling the snug pouches at the back of the mind,

and that one narrow finger grubbing, rat-a-tat,
for your soft spot. They never stop. They belong to you
and they will wait for you – in the borders of the wet garden,
the silence behind the beech hedge. They hoard rubber balls
and the past and all your lost things, and always want to know
when you're coming back, when you're coming back, when.

The Incredible Mrs Fox

You can fill the vase with as many cotters
of lavender as you like, but nothing will mask his scat.

He drags in the dawn through a crack in the curtain,
light running over his chin slippery as cracked egg.

And you just can't open your eyes fully yet, see
him slink into bed, aftershaved in vixen sweat,

a silk cloak of dew spittled onto his coat. Those fires
he wove through Lyke Wake aren't quite dead, not yet.

The fur retracts slowly, his cheek bristles into your neck
bright as the slag in the pockets of his kecks on the floor,

waiting for a man to step in. It's a nightly surrender,
your lisk and lish, lick and lap, black feathers lodged

between incisor and gum raining onto your face, cuckoo-spit
on his lips soaping the questions off your tongue.

You kiss him with one eye firmly on the door and watch
the sensible woman you were skulk out to the landing.

The Omnivore

An elegant young olinguito
swung down from the trees into Quito.
   She extended her paw
   to the first man she saw
and purred 'Pass me a god-damn mojito.'

On 15th August 2013 scientists announced
the discovery of a new mammal, the olinguito
(*Bassaricyon neblina*), in the Andes.

PART 2

The *Whole* King Kong Experience

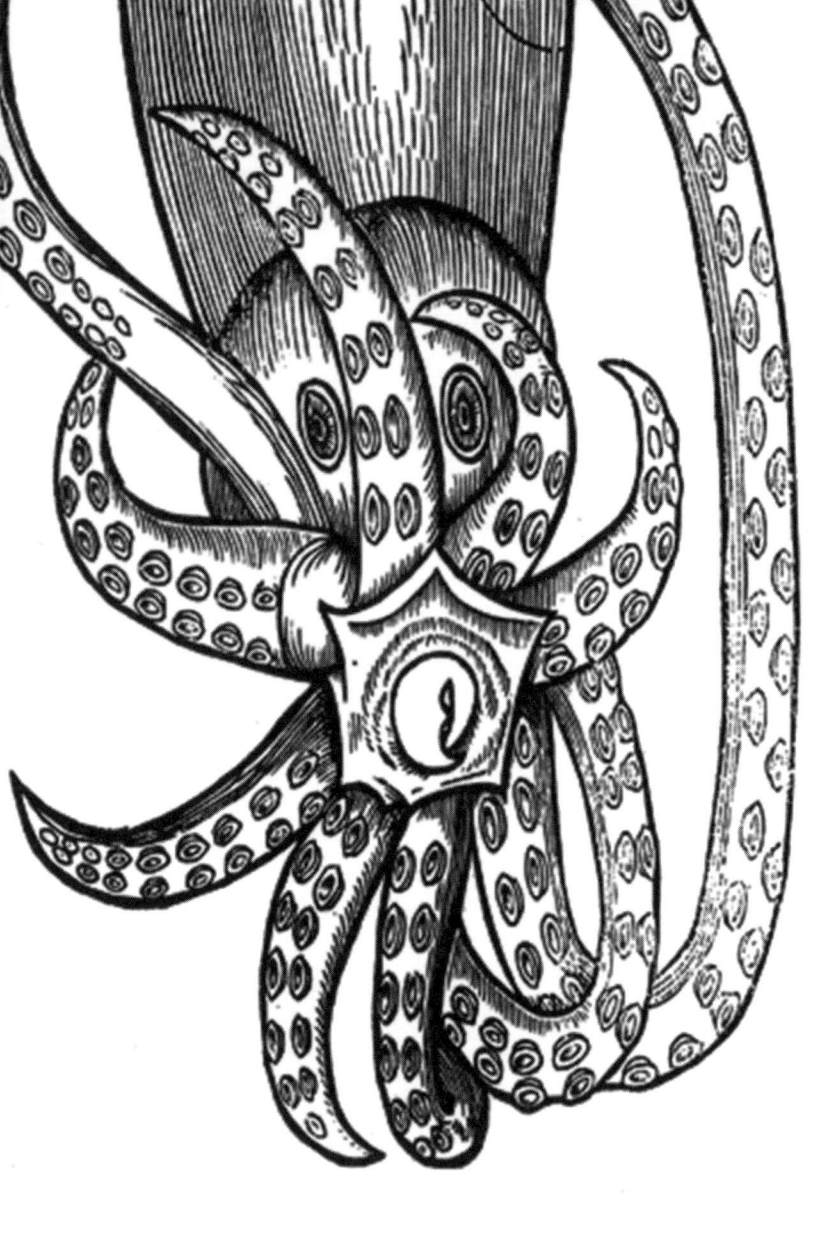

Frilled Lizard

You may think
   he's hungry for crickets
and that's why

he's tapping
   the vivarium glass
with his delicate claw

but you'd be wrong
   go on – slide open
the door

place your finger
   under his pouchy jaw
tickle his skin

watch how he settles
   how he curves his mouth
into a blissful grin

no, there's no need
   to wear gloves
he won't put up a fight

he may be cold to the touch
   but inside
he's alight.

Documentary on the Pangolin

She is how
we imagine
ourselves   as lovers:
                hunched and
                hardened – the
                head-down
                advance,   poised as if
                                to defuse a bomb.
                Like a monk   with a clasped haul
                of keys, leaning to unlock the termite
                mound and cover the body in insect
                vengeance. But   the pangolin
                is also

a fortress;
she can shoulder
such a siege. These   armour plates
could be kiln-   fired. She is a piglet
pinecone.   Her name in Indonesian:
          trenggiling, the sound
          collaborating, of a
               assembling
of tank-treads
shield formation
along the hillside
on the border   of the heart's
deepest   territory, as the tongue
          collects these black morsels
          by the dozen, extending stickily
          into every nook of the nest.
          Like us, she coils around
               the dragon-treasure

that is
her own soft
centre.

SANDRA HORN

Slug

All night
 I shall labour,
  as fast as
   I'm able.
  I'll beautify
   your paving,
    paint your
lawn, with
silvery
 messages
  of hope
   and joy.
    I'll sculpt
     as many
     leaves
      as I can
      reach
     (a large
    and most
    surprising
    number)
   to make
  exquisite
 filigrees,
through
which
 the moon

may shine,
the rosy
morning
gleam.
At last,
exhausted,
I shall seek
my bed
in the cool
damp
beneath
the shed.
I ask no
thanks,
no praise –
only that
you pause
a while,
reflect
upon my
work and
smile.

GABRIELLE TURNER

i, scarab

i am dor beetle, i am scarab,
the forest's senior waste management technician.
i'd just punched out, was walking home
and then this happened –
what a day, i'll tell them.

*Catapulted by a blackbird hop,
an almost-pebble gleams jewel-blue
in the dust, flipped like a shiny penny.
Heads you make it, tails you don't
and it's your lucky day: she'll flutter
you sideways in a puff of leaf-litter
before the footstep-rumbles come,
just in time.*

i pick forward, one leg less,
perhaps, or a little shaken up.
with thighs like mine i could have run
this wood, father used to say; not now.
but still, these biceps. swagger.
i'll sleep it off.

Fossa

There is a beast that runs
naked through the streets,
setting fire to bins,
trying on clothes in stores,

dresses she drops on the pavement
as passers-by gawk,

who throws coins at the crowds
and offers credit cards to kids.

Her tail is long as her body
and helps keep her balanced
as she climbs the stone trunks
of strange cities.

When she was ten
she could fight off gangs,
win every cat-fight,

could skip along jagged-glass walls
as they jeered about her mammy.

When rats leapt over her bed
she caught them.

Now, the doctors ask her who she is
and she says:
I am the fierce fossa
of Madagascar,

*I eat your cats and dogs,
my red tail is a torch
that sets fire to your cars.*

They ask her again,
as she races around
their consulting rooms.

They keep asking
until she gives the right answer.

Cryptoprocta ferox she bawls
in that voice she keeps for emergencies
like all the males are after her
and she's not ready.

Wrong! They shout, *wrong!*

They shave her red-brown fur
these he-doctors
and again she tries to escape,
to scale the towers of Liverpool, Cardiff…

Still she insists she's the ferocious spirit
of the Kirindy Forest,
the last daughter of her species.

They ask: *Who tamed you?*

She sits on the chair
and growls at the ghost
that's always there

following her down the cobbled alleys.

The Roach, she says, *that
playboy, lie-a-bed*

*who fucked the world
while I worked,*

*who tore into me
before I reached the mating tree,*

*before I offered myself
on the bridal branch, the high one
where I could kick off ugly suitors.*

Zebra on East 55th and 3rd

Unfazed, he grazes on popcorn and nachos
from a *Keep New York City Clean* litter bin,
shrouded in a canopy of cloud that leaches
through the steel bars of a subway vent.

Sneakered commuters steam by, too busy
to notice, too drunk on mobile devices.
Outside P.J. Clarke's a woman's whistle
lassos a yellow cab, hoists it kerbside.

Brooklyn, she snorts to the Iraqi driver.
The zebra lifts obsidian eyes, squints
at the transaction, the tap of a Yankees cap
and brays. His tail flicks sparks

at the dark carcass of a neon sign advertising
 old Beer by a 24-hour liquor store. It lights up.
He trots to the pedestrian crossing,
waits for *walk* to burn white and vanishes.

Snowflea Migration

We are nobodies, each a few millimetres
or so but high-spirited, hopping,
and yet obscure in our petty performing,
we sometimes travel en masse to fill
out a "we", tremulous, brimming
like a glass of water nearly spilling,
no, more like a ball rolling overland,
a half million, a million, above,
aslant, amid, springing, creeping,
seething through leaf litter and warmed
by the sun that with a grand gesture
exhorts and ignores us, discarded and guided
by the sun among weeds and melting snow,
our multitudes bivouac beside your boot,
on the field of your hovering hand the pepper
dots appear and disappear,
and who will say our two-day hadj,
perfected by a secret dispersion,
is profitless in every world

CHERYL MOSKOWITZ

Pond Requiem

I've known strange birds like this,
sleek feathered and inky black,
woven arms outstretched

like this giant sea raven forever
beating the air with his wings.
Will they never dry? I've seen

the old heron waiting patiently
after her kind before following
the lapwing – *deeds, not words*

embroidered in their flight, bright
sweep of green and purple
in the chill November sky.

I've watched white gulls pretending
to be doves, a couple cavorting
in the cold winter sun, shrill

scolds and screeches imitating love.
I've swum naked with them all
frozen and pale amongst the feathers

and fallen leaves. We are all mourners
here: the pairing gulls, one facing forward
the other back; the shivering egret

marble grey and stick thin waiting
for that glint of colour she knows
will disappear when day goes;

and you, mighty Cormoran
flapping your black funereal
gown in slow continuous motion.

The mighty will fall, boasts
killer Jack, *and none, not one,
will be coming back.*

Let's winter here together, friend,
for none of us can know our end.

Lesser flamingo

This need, so long out of season,
humbles me. Everything in me

contracts in preparation for winter,
for extremes. There is acid

in the lake. Birds in the lake.
Silt and salt and ice in the lake.

And I will wait for the algal bloom,
for you to see me, pink in the joints,

about the eyes. The bloom, when we
grow dark and cluster, pack into each

other and display our thin necks,
our straining beaks. The bloom when

I will call, and you will prepare
a place on your back for me.

Ladybird

Ladybirds when they fly reveal their hidden wings
of fine transparency, filigree netted underthings
beneath the flouncing polka dotted shell.
It is a game to count the spots, cupping hands around
in the hope she will not leave as she is so beautiful
but it is always when she wants to go
that the red skirt is raised and what is secret
delicately lifts her, swiftly taking her away.

Lapwings in Fallowfield

They sit with the road's oily
tang in their nares,
their bodies like helmets in grass.

Younger ones look like soil
upon snow and nest
in the adults' thick feathers.

My sister and I at somebody's
wedding, when we hid
under somebody's dress.

Romance in New Jersey

In May I sometimes think of the horseshoe crabs
gathering in mobs in the bay at Highland
where ferries leave for the city: the way
they come back year after year to begin
more horseshoe crabs, how they aren't really
crabs at all but ancient kin to the spider.
When I hitched up my skirt once and waded in
they parted gently to give me passage.

Under the moon is their time to dance,
ruled by the tides I've been told, but I prefer
the romance of it, their dull brown bodies
turning to gold in the water, their eight legs
reaching to hold each other in clumsy embrace
for days on end while commuters sail to Manhattan.

PART 3
Fins That Could Be Wings

Hare

> after a ceramic hare in a gallery

Unlike the fecund and promiscuous
rabbit whose offspring from numerous mothers
wander like sink estate kids

Hare leans on the boxing ring rope
fatalistic contempt on his face
takes his time as he watches his spar.

His gloves are polished as conkers.
His gaze seems to rest on a dream he once had
but his eyes measure distance and chance.

His muscles are tight as fired clay.
His pelt gleams with rain and his muzzle
gives nothing away.

Macbeth

crows whose wings are torn with wind
crows who croak the evening in
crows who dagger
crows who glare
crows and grey light everywhere

crows at vigil, candlelit
crows who bow their blackened beaks
crows as watchers
crows as witch
crows as bent and burnt as wicks

crows that banquet, gullet wide
crows that feast on bleating eyes
crows as dead man
crows in clans
crows in ghosts and knives and lambs

Build

There won't be a manual.
Don't expect instructions to be etched,
as scrimshaw, on a tooth.
Don't panic-flick through *Moby-Dick*.
Think benthic.

Begin with the insides.
Don't try to refine the design –
just bear in mind, as you loop
          and wind
   its quarter-
               mile of intestines,
that you'll need to add an enzyme
which can form chyme from plastic.

Though you'll flail many times, waist-deep
in spermaceti, you must never fail
to grin. A frown
will rigidify collapsible ribs;
a curse could shift   blowhole
     to fin.

When straining to start its skiff-sized heart,
cling, like a giant squid, to your task,
till your will inflicts suction cup marks
on its rippling Pacific of skin.

Make sure you've got thrash metal blaring
as you fill it with clicks
       and breath
              on the off-chance
that this'll prepare it for decades of drilling
and seismic tests.

Be ready for the moment when it outknows you,
when the weight of its brain takes over
and goads you
to renovate yourself.

MAGGIE SAWKINS

The Zoo Keeper's Song

I could watch them for hours
Esmeralda and Zola
strolling up and down
on legs as long as stilted circus clowns.
With my daily offerings
of lettuce, radish and grape
I enter the enclosure
run my hand over
the primitive patchwork skin
watch how they flutter their eyelashes
like two actresses
in an old time movie.

When I come back
I want to be the leaves
of the tallest trees.
I want to be devoured
by those magnificent tongues.

JACQUELINE SAPHRA

Family Viewing

Each time Good Penguin
leaves his gaff-in-progress,

Bad Penguin takes
another pebble from his stash.

Good Penguin labours
without a break, chooses

his materials with care.
This sombre task absorbs him,

focused, as he is, on
nesting matters; how to make

a home that's full and rounded
in this desolation.

My children on the sofa
cheer for him, lone hero:

I know he'll never win.
Bad Penguin's really bad;

Good Penguin doesn't cotton on.
Why can't he count?

He doesn't notice that his nest,
which should be chic

and sumptuous, is so much
smaller than the rest

and in this icy pantomime,
he's back and forth

with pebbles in his beak;
but who will want him now,

his genome demonstrably
weak, his crib diminished?

Meanwhile, Bad Penguin
builds from stolen hoards;

with this capacious pile
he'll have his pick of mates,

his line's assured.
My children watch the plot

unfold: it's hard to read
their laughter. Soon

they scatter and are gone.
The credits roll, I plump

the cushions, draw the curtains
tight against the cold.

SHAUNA ROBERTSON

The Fish without a Bicycle

has, since early roe-hood, pictured the
   freedom of the towpath
on two wheels,

coveted handlebars
like a carp possessed
of the arms to seize,

harboured a penchant for pedals
like a perch with no rest
and busting with the urge

to crest dry horizons poised
on a high hard seat
that so pummels the would-be buttocks

one has to wonder,
when was the last time
I felt such a thirst?

Ordeal by Water

> *water shal refuse to receive them in her bosom, that*
> *have shaken off them the sacred Water of Baptisme,*
> *and wilfullie refused the benefite thereo*
>
> King James I, *Daemonologie* (1597)

She'd bid the malkin to the house,
and it had waxed grotesque in size
these past weeks

and hence the Devil juggled their false shadows
until his wife and her black creature
were supernaturally conjoined.

And now that monster slept diagonal
across the marriage bed
while the farm was havocked barren.

So he wrangled up that monstrous cat,
bound it, thrice ducked it in the pond.
When it sank he knew he loved her.

His Catherine with her starless hair;
her milk pan skin;
unwitched and twice baptised.

Reynard

Big old dog fox,
heavy with health,
with cock.
       The balls on you!
Curled up there, brassy in the sun.

I'd like to take hold of your snout,
feel the squeak
       of your teeth
against my thumb.
            Borrow your coat awhile,
      big old dog fox.

How long do you suppose before I'd turn?

Take to dossing on compost,
            hoodwinking crows.
    Stinky, hungry
for what it is that makes you blush.
Your cunning about my shoulders,
      quick words
rising in my throat.

            How long before I'd take
a foot to the itch behind my ribs?
Forget this knife,
      this aubergine dish.

How d'ya like them apples?

And then of course, there was the incident
    with a trout; that three pound Paperbelle
I pulled from Lake Superior, while you were running for salmon.

And I just loved it – the catching of it and the thing itself.
    Luxurious in its brown and gold skin, like that beautiful handbag
        I should have bought, instead of a plane ticket.

And that delicious boy, the blue charter boat, the white smile;
    he laughed with me as his nets uncoiled their orangey knots
        and he knelt with me on the hopelessly wet deck to hold
the trout; my feathery trout with eyes that shone like nothing ever had.

I stayed out on the blue boat, stayed out all afternoon;
    sailed back to the quay with empty hands and salt in my hair.

    Some things cannot be explained; some creatures
swim, others breathe and some cannot be caught.

Myxomatosis, 1970s

We found a rabbit –
crazy – lolloping
in the trees with
sightless eyes
in a swollen head.
The merciful thing
was to end its
life right then.
Kick it hard or
bash its brains out.
We hung it
spinning from
a branch and hit it
with a stick –
sending it
into orbit,
till its body split
in two, spraying
a Catherine wheel
of blood and liquid
rabbit shit
that covered us
in reek and gunge
that stayed with us
for weeks.
This happened.
I was there.

Are we there yet?

On the drive from Des Moines, deer along the highway's
gravel shoulder. Deer's eyes flaring
from corridors of corn.

Lithe, narrow-faced silhouettes of deer
beneath rare mosquito-swarmed streetlights,
more numerous than the streetlights

floating above alfalfa, soybeans, hay,
the grid of roads dividing fields from fields.
Death is like the softest scarf settling

over your face. My grandfather knew this
because he'd died a year before he died.
He'd felt it, wasn't afraid. That night

the deer were spirits drifting, foraging, so many
souls of the damned. Hundreds surfaced
as you drove, and twice

I saw the handkerchief drifting down
from heaven, felt it brush my eyes,
my chin. A yearling first,

and, miles later, a sharp-racked buck, leapt
onto the road in front of the car, the larger
it seemed right over the ticking hood.

Death is silk, is cashmere. It wasn't how
I wanted us to end. Didn't we
make it to sunrise? I thought so,

I was certain. I remember the dew across the even stalks
like sheets of muslin, the phosphorescent lake
hung with mist.

Kyril's Tale

Is it true? they ask as he limps back from the bog, gobs into a steel spittoon,
settles into his seat by the stove. True? Of course it's true,
true as the boils on my mother's arse: buy me one and I'll tell you the story.

One autumn, we're in Poznań awaiting the visit of a Party Boss,
whose staff have declared wants to shoot a bear, the comrades to arrange it.
A bear, he growls, the bastard wanted to shoot a bear.

So after much vodka, some bright spark who still had the power of speech
says let's commandeer a circus bear, install it in a hut deep in the forest.
A circus bear, he grunts, sinking his slivovitz – problem sorted.

When said bigshot arrives, all epaulettes and entourage
of apparatchik arse-lickers – says if things go well, a new house, a car –
he's told we hunt at dawn.

So we're out in the birch woods freezing our bollocks off,
tracking this bear turfed out of his hut for the sake of diplomatic relations –
who's running through the trees, bewildered by our shouts,

bullets whistling past his snout, finally we catch sight of him standing
on the far side of a clearing watching some old guy cycling up a forest track.
'Course that bear knows all about bicycles. Next thing we know

he's haring after the old guy, who leaps off his bike, the bear leaps on,
builds up a head of steam and cycles off through the trees leaving us in stunned silence –
wondering if we're about to head east for a nice little holiday.

But no. The big man laughs so hard he nearly wets himself. And we join in.
The rest's a blur, but later, before passing out at the Pravoskaya
I remember worrying about that bear, if his wild kin accepted him

once the smell of sawdust faded from his fur.
There you have it, he growls and smacks his hand on the table –
a tale from the good old days.

Chimpanzee Burial at Sanaga-Yong Rescue Centre

poem found in a newspaper article

She had been sold as a baby.
Kept tethered for twenty-five years.
Taught to drink beer and smoke cigarettes.

She spent her last eight years
at Sanaga-Yong.
Her kindness surfaced,

she mothered an orphan,
befriended others.

Dorothy died of a heart attack.

At her burial, some barked
in frustration but
the most stunning reaction
was a recurring, almost tangible
silence –

Martha, The Last Passenger Pigeon

Last of the good time girls – sure she liked a drink,
knew how to make a party swing, how to
string a guy along until the pivotal moment.

Lipstick fires in her feathers; the smoky
turn of her neck as she came into a room.
Who knew where she was going to, and
what's a girl like that got to do with settling down?

Cincinnati couldn't hold me, she liked to say.
I was never a bird in a gilded cage and
Why the hell shouldn't youth play with age?

Remember her as she always intended to be:
out of a sky that once held a billion others
the one who stood out from the crowd.

The last known North American passenger pigeon died in Cincinnati Zoo in 1914. Attempts to mate her with the last two surviving males had failed. It is estimated that there were around 5 billion passenger pigeons in North America when European settlers first arrived.

ACKNOWLEDGEMENTS

'Scorpion', by Sharon Black, was previously published in her collection *The Art of Egg* (Two Ravens Press, 2015).

'Myxomatosis, 1970s', by Tim Cresswell, was previously published in his collection *Soil* (Penned in the Margins, 2013).

'Snowflea Migration', by Philip Fried, was previously published in his collection *Early/Late: New and Selected Poems* (Salmon Poetry, Ireland, 2011).

'Lapwings in Fallowfield', by Katherine Horrex, was first published by *The Manchester Review* on their website in December 2017 and also appears in Carcanet's *New Poetries VII*, published in April 2018.

'Zebra on East 55th and 3rd', by Ian Humphreys, was previously published in *Poetry News* in 2015 and then on The Poetry Society's website in 2016 after it won the Hamish Canham Prize that year.

'Ladybird', by Emma McKervey, was first published in her collection *The Rag Tree Speaks* (Doire Press, 2017).

'The Lemures', by Abigail Parry, was previously published in her collection *Jinx* (Bloodaxe, 2018).

'Fossa' and 'My Wolverine', by Pascale Petit, were both previously published in her collection *Mama Amazonica* (Bloodaxe, 2017).

'Hare', by Pauline Plummer, first appeared in her collection *Bint* (Red Squirrel Press, 2011).

'Boy', by Stav Poleg, was previously published in *Gutter Magazine* (Issue 13, Summer 2015).

'Gorilla', by Mel Pryor, was previously published in her

collection *Small Nuclear Family* (Eyewear, 2015).

'Build', by Susan Richardson, was previously published in *The Hopper* (Green Writers Press, Issue II, 2017) and in her collection *Words the Turtle Taught Me* (Cinnamon Press, 2018).

'The Fish without a Bicycle', by Shauna Robertson, was previously published in her pamphlet *Blueprints for a Minefield* (Fair Acre Press, 2016).

'The Zoo Keeper's Song', by Maggie Sawkins, was previously published in her collection *The Zig Zag Woman* (Two Ravens Press, 2007).

'Frilled Lizard', by Maggie Sawkins, was previously published in *Extraordinary Forms* (Queen's Park Books, 2016).

'How d'ya like them apples?', by Rosie Shepperd, was previously published in her pamphlet *That so-easy thing* (smith|doorstop, 2013).

'Chimpanzee Burial at Sanaga-Yong Rescue Centre', by Degna Stone, was previously published in her collection *Record and Play* (Red Squirrel Press, 2015). The last stanza quotes the words of photographer Monica Szczupider.

'I Had a Brindled Cow' is an anonymous Latvian folk song. This translation by Bitite Vinklers was previously published in *Words Without Borders* in 2006.

'Reynard', by Ruth Wiggins, was previously published in her pamphlet *Myrtle* (Emma Press, 2014).

ABOUT THE EDITORS

Anja Konig grew up in the German language and now writes in English. Her first pamphlet, *Advice for an Only Child*, was shortlisted for the 2015 Michael Marks Award. Anja is working on her next collection of poems, *Animal Experiments*. She is a scientist by training and has long been fascinated by human primates and other creatures.

Liane Strauss is an American poet and professor of Comparative Literature and Creative Writing. She is the author of three poetry collections: *Frankie, Alfredo,* (Donut Press, 2009), *Leaving Eden* (Salt Publishing, 2010), and *All the Ways You Still Remind Me of the Moon* (Paekakariki Press, 2015). Liane teaches at NYU, participates regularly in *The Hudson Review*'s Writers in the Schools, and holds an active Research Fellowship at Goldsmiths, University of London. She is currently looking for a US publisher for her most recently completed manuscript of poems, *Prodigal*, working on a new collection of poems, and beginning to circulate her first novel, *The Other Side of You*, to agents.

ABOUT THE AUTHORS

Kathleen Moran Bainbridge has worked as a singer, teacher and Gestalt therapist. In 2014 she was runner-up for the Flambard Prize and in 2015 she won a New Writing North award. Her poems have appeared in magazines, anthologies and online. She lives across a ford in Northumberland.

Sharon Black is from Scotland but now lives in the mountains of the south of France, where scorpions are a welcome but infrequent occurrence. She has two collections: *To Know Bedrock* (Pindrop Press, 2011) and *The Art of Egg* (Two Ravens Press, 2015). www.sharonblack.co.uk

Victoria Briggs is an award-winning, Pushcart-nominated writer of poetry and short fiction, with work published in *The Stockholm Review, Structo, The Honest Ulsterman, Unthology, Litro, Prole, Short Fiction* and *The Jellyfish Review*. She lives in London, where she's writing a novel, and tweets @vicbriggs.

Nancy Campbell's books include *How To Say 'I Love You' In Greenlandic: An Arctic Alphabet*, which won the Birgit Skiöld Award in 2013, and *Disko Bay* (Enitharmon, 2015), which was shortlisted for the Forward Prize for Best First Collection in 2016. www.nancycampbell.co.uk

Tim Cresswell is a geographer-poet. He is the author of two collections published by Penned in the Margins: *Soil* (2013) and *Fence* (2015). He lives in West Hartford, Connecticut with his wife Carol, daughter Maddy, and three cats, Quin, Leo and Brie.

Maggie Dietz's two books of poems are *That Kind of Happy* and *Perennial Fall*. She is Associate Professor at the University of Massachusetts Lowell.

Philip Fried has published seven books of poetry, most recently *Squaring the Circle* (Salmon Poetry, 2017). His collection *Interrogating Water* (Salmon, 2014) was called 'outstanding' by Carol Rumens in the *Guardian*. 'Snowflea Migration' is from a series of poems in the voices of insects.

Gregg Friedberg is the author of *The Best Seat Not in the House* (Main Street Rag, 2010; Embajadoras Press, 2017), a poem sequence concerning the relations between creator and creature, and *Would You Be Made Whole?* (Aldrich Press, 2015), a collection of 'unruly' sonnets.

David Hale has a pamphlet from HappenStance and another from Templar. He has a lurcher, a ginger tom and a chestnut mare and enjoys the company of animals.

Sarah Hesketh holds an MA in Creative Writing from UEA. In 2013 she was poet-in-residence with Age Concern, working with elderly people with dementia, and in 2014 she published *The Hard Word Box* (Penned in the Margins), a collection of poems and interviews inspired by this experience.

Sandra Horn is an award-winning children's author based in Southampton. She has had poems commissioned by BBC Active Schools' history programmes and has been published in *Magma* and *Artemis* poetry magazines and in *The Emma Press Anthology of Age*.

Katherine Horrex's poems have featured in the *Times Literary Supplement*, *Morning Star*, and *PN Review*, among others. Her work has also been anthologised in *Introduction X* (The Poetry Business, 2017) and most recently in *New Poetries VII* (Carcanet, 2018).

Ian Humphreys has been widely published in journals including *Ambit, The Poetry Review* and *The Rialto*. In 2016, he won the Hamish Canham Prize and was selected for The Complete Works III. A portfolio of his poems features in *TEN: Poets of the New Generation* (Bloodaxe, 2017).

Helen Ivory's fourth Bloodaxe collection is *Waiting for Bluebeard*. She edits the webzine *Ink Sweat and Tears* and is tutor and course director for the UEA/WCN Creative Writing programme. Her collection *The Anatomical Venus* is forthcoming from Bloodaxe.

Russell Jones is an Edinburgh-based writer and editor. He has published four collections of poetry and edited two writing anthologies. He is deputy editor of *Shoreline of Infinity,* a science fiction magazine. He has a PhD in Creative Writing from The University of Edinburgh.

Donika Kelly's first poetry collection *BESTIARY* (Graywolf, 2016) was the winner of the 2015 Cave Canem Poetry Prize. She received her MFA in Writing from the Michener Center for Writers and a PhD in English from Vanderbilt University. She is an Assistant Professor at St. Bonaventure University.

Eve Lacey is from Brighton and lives in Cambridge, where she works as a librarian. She is the editor of *Furies* (For Books' Sake, 2014), and *The Emma Press Anthology of the Sea* (2016). In 2017, she was a poet-in-residence at Addenbrooke's hospital.

Emma McKervey's debut collection *The Rag Tree Speaks* was published in 2017 by Doire Press. Her poems have been shortlisted for the Irish Poem of the Year (2016) and the FSNI National Poetry Competition (2016) and highly commended in the Seamus Heaney New Writing Prize in 2017.

Cheryl Moskowitz was born in Chicago and grew up among the foothills of the Rocky Mountains in Denver, Colorado. She writes for adults and children. Her publications include *The Girl is Smiling* (Circle Time Press, 2012) and *Can it Be About Me?* (Frances Lincoln, 2012).

Abigail Parry's first collection, *Jinx*, is published by Bloodaxe, and features lemurs, lizards, moths, minnows, corvids, reedlings, a wolf, a hare, a shark, a snake and a sexy goat.

Pascale Petit's seventh collection, *Mama Amazonica* (Bloodaxe, 2017), was a Poetry Book Society Choice and draws on her travels in the Amazon rainforest. Her sixth, *Fauverie*, was her fourth to be shortlisted for the T. S. Eliot Prize and five poems from it won the Manchester Poetry Prize. In 2015 she received a Cholmondeley Award.

Pauline Plummer is an Irish/Welsh mixture from Liverpool who has lived in the North East since the 80s. Her last full collection was *Bint* (Red Squirrel Press, 2011). She has also published short stories and a verse novella *From Here to Timbuktu* (Smokestack Press, 2012).

Stav Poleg's poetry has appeared in *The New Yorker, Poetry London,* and *Poetry Ireland Review*. Her graphic-novel installation, *Dear Penelope: Variations on an August Morning*, with artist Laura Gressani, was acquired by the Scottish National Gallery of Modern Art. She lives in Cambridge, UK.

Mel Pryor has won the Essex Poetry Prize, the Ware Sonnet Prize and the Philip Larkin Poetry Prize. She has published two books with Eyewear: a pamphlet, *Drawn on Water* (2014), and a full collection, *Small Nuclear Family* (2015), which was described in the *TLS* as 'a remarkable debut'.

Angela Readman has won the Mslexia and Essex poetry competitions and the Charles Causley Award. Her latest collection is *The Book of Tides* (Nine Arches, 2016) and her debut story collection *Don't Try This at Home* (And Other Stories, 2015) won The Rubery Book Award.

Susan Richardson is a poet, performer and educator whose fourth collection of poetry, *Words the Turtle Taught Me*, has just been published by Cinnamon Press. She is currently poet-in-residence with both the global animal welfare initiative, World Animal Day, and the British Animal Studies Network. www.susanrichardsonwriter.co.uk

Shauna Robertson's poems have been set to music, displayed on buses, made into comic art, hung on a pub wall, and published in various lit mags and anthologies. She has two chapbooks: *Blueprints for a Minefield* and *Hack*. Shauna also writes for children and makes artwork.

Jacqueline Saphra's recent pamphlets are *If I Lay on my Back I Saw Nothing but Naked Women* (Emma Press, 2014) and *A Bargain with the Light: Poems after Lee Miller* (Hercules Editions, 2017). Her latest collection, *All My Mad Mothers* (Nine Arches, 2017), was shortlisted for the T.S. Eliot prize.

Maggie Sawkins is the winner of the 2013 Ted Hughes Award for New Work in Poetry. She lives in Portsmouth and is involved in writing projects in community and healthcare settings. www.hookedonwords.wordpress.com

Rosie Shepperd's collection *The Man at the Corner Table* (Seren) was published in 2015. Her poem 'A seedy narrative or moments of lyrical stillness?' was shortlisted for the Forward Prize for Best Single Poem in 2013. She is currently finishing a PhD at Goldsmiths.

Saliann St-Clair obtained a first in the BA Creative Writing programme at Birkbeck, University of London. She is a London-born, psychotically calm, functioning anaemic who writes, sings, travels, camps indoors and eats cake. She is a content writer for an online magazine, and is working on her first novel and first collection of poems.

Degna Stone is co-founder of *Butcher's Dog* poetry magazine and a contributing editor at *The Rialto*. She received a Northern Writers' Award in 2015, holds an MA in Creative Writing from Newcastle University and is a fellow of The Complete Works.

Jon Stone previously co-edited the four-volume *Birdbook* anthology series and *Aquanauts*, a compendium on underwater life and exploration (all published by Sidekick Books). He is also co-author of a book of tropical animal sonnets, *Riotous*, which won a Saboteur Award for Best Collaboration. He owns a soft toy cheetah called Quickstep.

Gabrielle Turner is a writer, editor and translator living where Surrey, Berkshire and Hampshire converge. When she's not writing poems and stories you'll find her exploring forests and riverbanks, sculpting creatures out of clay or indulging the whims of her mostly upside-down greyhound.

Bitite Vinklers is a translator of Latvian folklore and contemporary literature. Her translations have appeared in anthologies and journals, including *The Paris Review, Subtropics* and *Words Without Borders*. Recent work includes Imants Ziedonis, *Each Day Catches Fire: Poems* (Red Dragonfly Press, 2015), and Knuts Skujenieks, *Seed in Snow: Poems* (BOA Editions, 2016).

Ruth Wiggins lives in London. Her poems have appeared most recently in *POETRY, The Poetry Review, Long Poem Magazine* and *The Wolf*. Her pamphlet *Myrtle* (Emma Press, 2014) was runner-up in the Fledgling Poetry Award. She blogs at mudpath.wordpress.com

ABOUT THE EMMA PRESS

small press, big dreams

☙❧

The Emma Press is an independent publisher dedicated to producing beautiful, thought-provoking books. It was founded in 2012 by Emma Wright in Winnersh and is now based in Birmingham.

Having been shortlisted in both 2014 and 2015, the Emma Press won the Michael Marks Award for Poetry Pamphlet Publishers in 2016.

The Emma Press is passionate about publishing literature which is welcoming and accessible. Sign up to the Emma Press newsletter to hear about upcoming events, publications and calls for submissions.

theemmapress.com
emmavalleypress.blogspot.co.uk

☙❧